love story of

&

"ONCE IN A WHILE,
RIGHT IN THE MIDDLE
OF AN ORDINARY LIFE,
LOVE GIVES US A
FAIRY TALE."

UNKNOWN AUTHOR

Scripture quotations are from

The ESV® Bible (The Holy Bible, English Standard Version®), copyright © 2001 by Crossway, a publishing ministry of Good News Publishers. Used by permission. All rights reserved.

The Holy Bible, New International Version®, NIV®. Copyright © 1973, 1978, 1984, 2011 by Biblica, Inc.® Used by permission. All rights reserved worldwide.

Cover and interior design by Nicole Dougherty

Artwork © 2017 Ginger Chen

WEDDED BLISS

Copyright © 2017 by Harvest House Publishers
Published by Harvest House Publishers
Eugene, Oregon 97402
www.harvesthousepublishers.com

ISBN 978-0-7369-6939-0

Printed in China

17 18 19 20 21 22 23 24 25 / RDS-JC / 10 9 8 7 6 5 4 3 2 1

WEDDED Bliss

HARVEST HOUSE PUBLISHERS
EUGENE, OREGON

NOW WHAT?

The wedding is over.
The preparations are finished.
The gifts have been unwrapped.
And the honeymoon is over.

Seriously, now what?

Now the real adventure begins!

This book will help you capture snippets of your
unique love story as you learn more about each
other and spend time together. Don't worry about
completing this book within a specific time frame.
Open it when you can, when you are thinking about
it—maybe on a date night or when you
are looking for something to do.

Not a newlywed? This book is for you too.
Delight in reliving some of the early moments
together and take an opportunity for some
intentional time together.

So have some fun and enjoy the journey!

Wedding Details

Date

Time

Location

Weather

Maid of Honor

Best Man

Colors

I do! Me too!

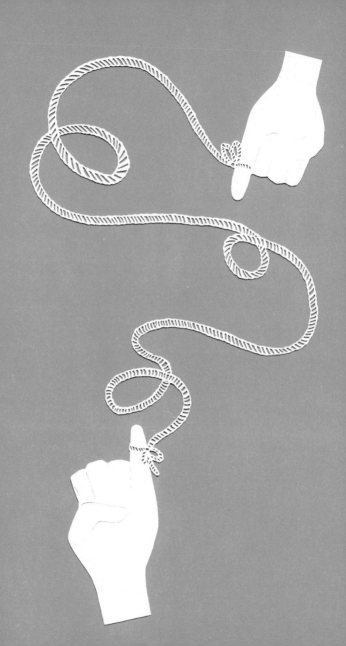

Love

BEARS ALL THINGS,
BELIEVES ALL THINGS,
HOPES ALL THINGS,
ENDURES ALL THINGS.
LOVE NEVER ENDS.

THE BOOK OF 1 CORINTHIANS

Share your favorite moment from your wedding.

HIS

Something always goes wrong at a wedding... What was it for you?

_Don't worry.
In time, you'll be able to laugh about this!_

WITH THAT RING I
GAVE YOU MY HEART.
I PROMISED FROM THAT
DAY FORWARD, YOU WOULD
NEVER WALK ALONE; MY HEART
WOULD BE YOUR SHELTER,
AND MY ARMS WOULD
BE YOUR HOME.

AUTHOR UNKNOWN

What song was playing
for your first dance?

_____

Write down your proposal story.

Get all the fun details. What went according to plan? Better yet, what didn't?

_____

_____

_____

_____

_____

_____

_____

_____

_____

_____

_____

_____

_____

_____

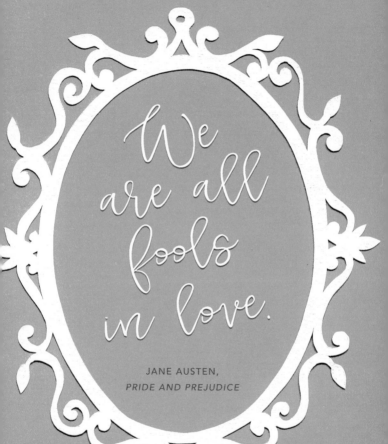

We
are all
fools
in love.

JANE AUSTEN,
PRIDE AND PREJUDICE

Describe how you felt during your
"first look" at the wedding.

HIS

If you could be any famous couple
from history, who would you be?

&

What has been the hardest
thing about being married?

It's okay—be honest!

What has been the best part of being married?

_____

_____

_____

_____

_____

_____

_____

_____

_____

_____

_____

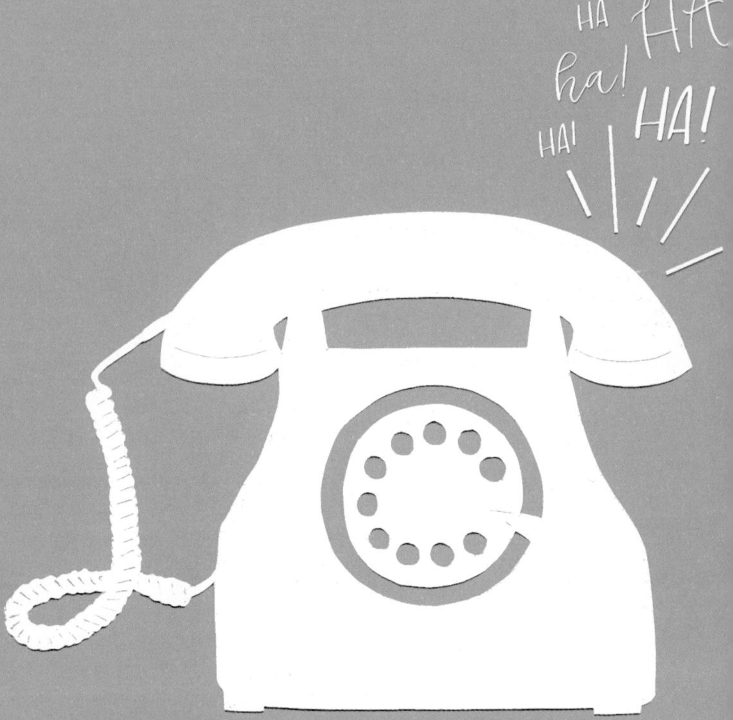
HA
HA
ha!
HA!
HA!

Record a time you both laughed so hard you cried.

_____

_____

_____

_____

_____

_____

_____

_____

_____

_____

_____

_____

_____

What was the first movie
you saw together?

_____

If you have the ticket stubs, tape them here.

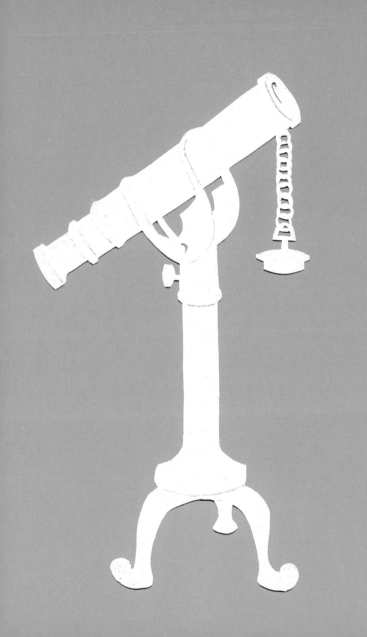

Reflect on all that had to go right for you and your spouse to find each other. Was it a chance meeting? Had you been friends for years? Or...

_____

_____

_____

_____

_____

_____

_____

_____

_____

_____

_____

_____

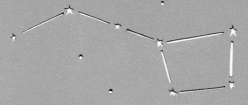

Where was your first kiss?

_____

_____

_____

If you can, go back and experience it again!

Where did you go
on your honeymoon?

*Tuck a ticket stub, brochure,
or silly memento in the book.*

Describe one of your favorite
moments on the honeymoon.

_____

_____

_____

_____

_____

_____

_____

_____

_____

_____

_____

His

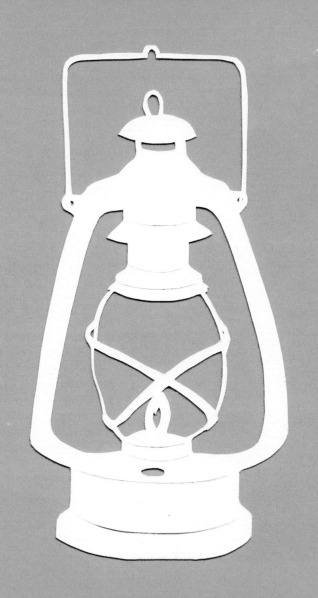

Love must be
as much a light,
as it is a flame.

HENRY DAVID THOREAU

At what point in your marriage
will you have been together longer
than you have been apart?

Make a note and plan something
special for that future date.

If your love story had a title,
what would it be?

_____

_____

_____

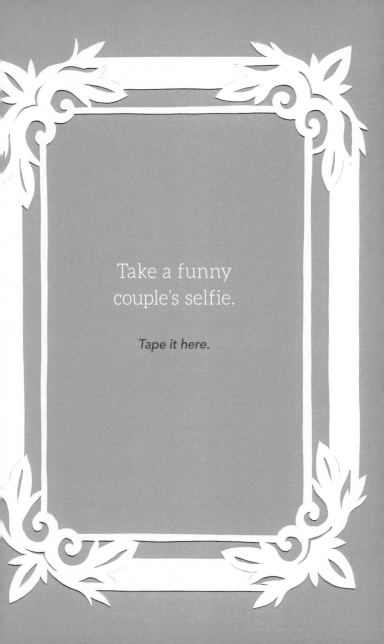

Take a funny
couple's selfie.

Tape it here.

Be a tourist in your own town.
What are the top five must-dos
in your area?

1. _____

2. _____

3. _____

4. _____

5. _____

*Do them together,
taking a picture together at each stop.
Tuck a few pictures between these pages.*

What gift, skill, or talent do you
most admire in your spouse?

_____

_____

_____

_____

_____

_____

HIS...

HERS...

If I
had a flower
for every time I
thought of you...

I could
walk through
my garden
forever.

ALFRED TENNYSON

Try a new cuisine together.
What did you order or cook?

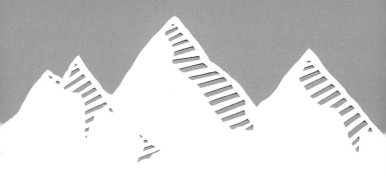

What's the craziest thing you
did when you were dating?

_____

_____

_____

Do it again!

How did you feel when you first
heard the words, *I love you?*

_____

_____

_____

_____

_____

_____

_____

_____

_____

_____

_____

HIS

In dreams
and in love
there are no
impossibilities.

JÁNOS ARANY

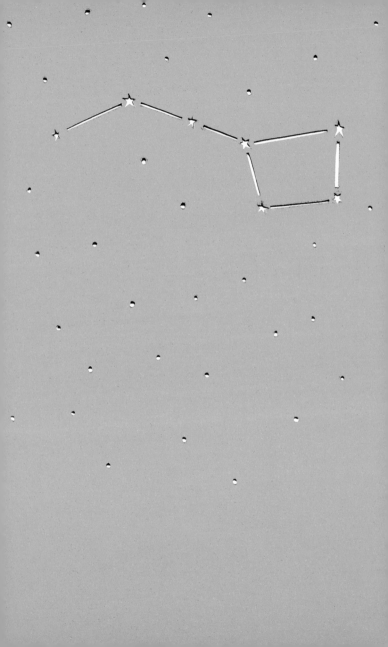

Take sleeping bags into your backyard and stargaze. Talk about your dreams for the future.

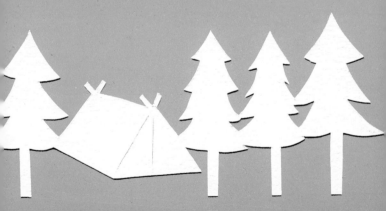

If your spouse was
a superhero, what would
his/her superpower be?

HIS

_____

_____

_____

_____

_____

_____

HERS

I am
my beloved's
and my beloved
is mine.

THE SONG OF SOLOMON

Go to your favorite restaurant and
commit to trying something new.
What did you have?

_____

_____

_____

Remember a time when you felt absolutely overwhelmed by love or appreciation for your spouse.

HIS

Find a local movie in the park
or at a drive-in and go!

Save the ticket stub between these pages.

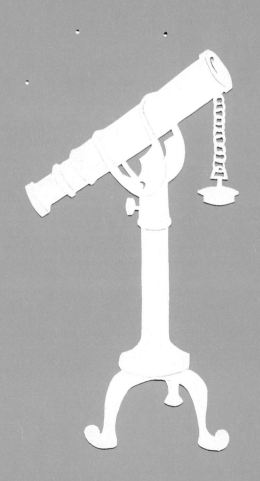

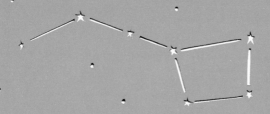

Take turns sharing a
favorite hobby or pastime
with your spouse.

WARNING: You might actually enjoy it!

WHATEVER
OUR SOULS
ARE MADE OF,
HIS AND MINE
ARE THE SAME.

EMILY BRONTË

Write down three things you love about your spouse.

1. _____

2. _____

3. _____

1. _____

2. _____

3. _____

*Come back to this page when you
have an argument. It will help.*

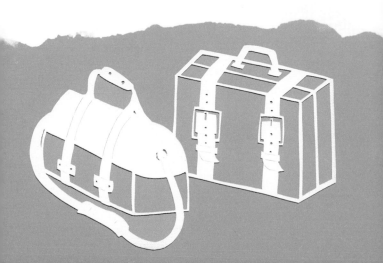

Re-create your first date.
Reminisce about your
first impressions.

Come on...dig deep for the embarrassing stuff.

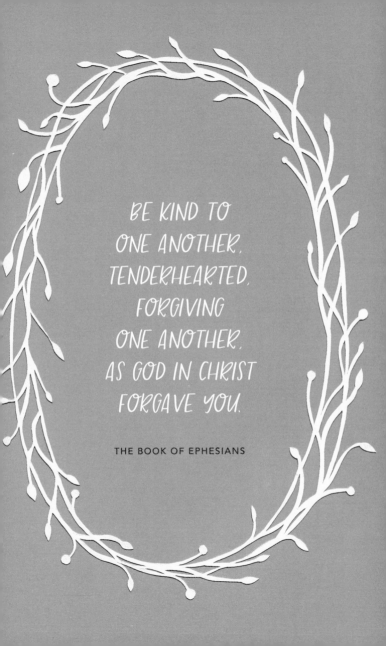

BE KIND TO
ONE ANOTHER,
TENDERHEARTED,
FORGIVING
ONE ANOTHER,
AS GOD IN CHRIST
FORGAVE YOU.

THE BOOK OF EPHESIANS

Pick a favorite old movie
and have a movie night together,
complete with popcorn, movie candy,
and a cozy blanket or fire.

What's your song?

_____

_____

_____

Don't have one? Pick one together now!

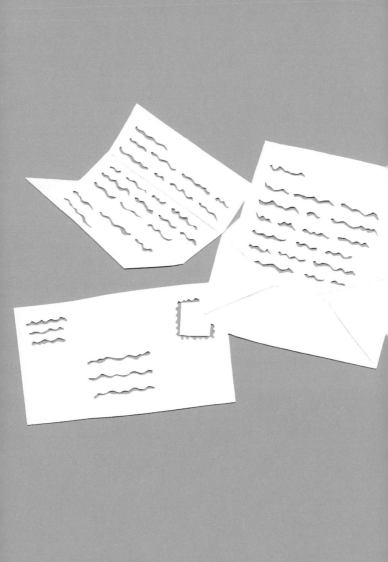

If you could give a piece of advice
to a couple that has just started
dating, what would it be?

_____

_____

_____

_____

_____

_____

_____

_____

_____

_____

_____

_____

Love

DOESN'T MAKE THE
WORLD GO 'ROUND;
LOVE IS WHAT MAKES
THE RIDE WORTHWHILE.

FRANKLIN P. JONES

Describe the moment you knew you had found "the one."

_____

_____

_____

_____

_____

_____

_____

_____

_____

_____

HIS

HERS

If you were to get his-and-her tattoos,
what designs would you choose?

Sketch them here.

So they are no longer two, but one flesh. Therefore what God has joined together, let no one separate.

THE BOOK OF MATTHEW

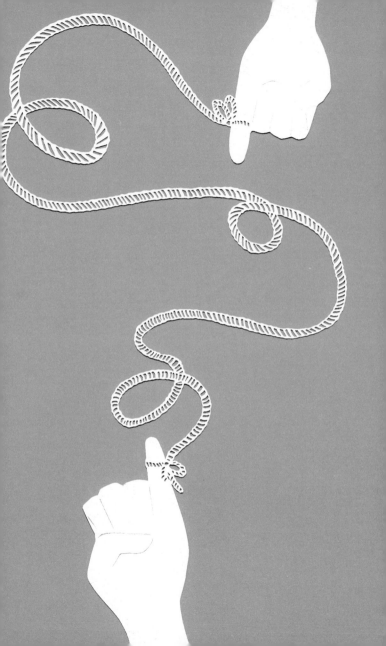

What is something you have
always wanted to learn to do?
Take a class together!

*Ideas: cooking, finger painting, pottery, guitar
lessons, interpretative dance, a language class…*

There is no
fear in love,
but perfect love
casts out fear.

THE BOOK OF 1 JOHN

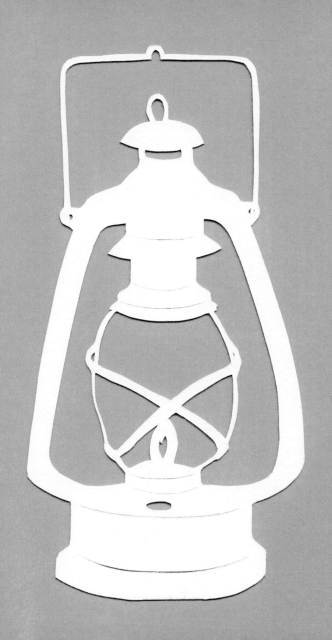

Do you want kids?
Write down some of your
favorite names.

_____

_____

_____

_____

_____

_____

_____

_____

_____

_____

If not... This just got awkward...

Create a playlist of favorite songs.
Then dim the lights and dance.

The greatest
achievement in my
life thus far has
been to love you and
be loved by you.

AUTHOR UNKNOWN

What is your dream vacation?

_____

Start a vacation fund by
designating a jar to collect
change and small bills.

*Your dream vacation could be a
reality sooner than you think.*

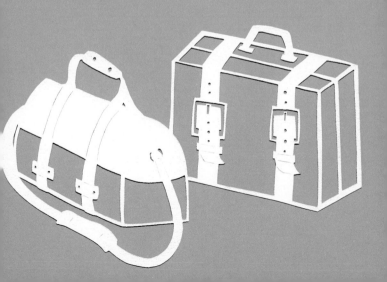

Host a themed costume party featuring famous literary, TV, or movie couples. Who did you choose to be?

_____ & _____

Take turns planning a "favorites" day for your spouse. Jot down his or her favorite foods, activities, pastimes, ways to relax, and so on. Put as many of them into the day as you can.

_____

_____

_____

_____

Complete a seven-day
"Why I Love You" texting challenge!

For the next seven days, text your
spouse a reason you love them.

Bonus points if you can make your partner laugh!

And walk in love,
as Christ loved us
and gave himself up
for us, a fragrant
offering and
sacrifice to God.

THE BOOK OF EPHESIANS

Pack a picnic and go all
out with your favorite foods.
Find a local park you have
never visited, spread out a
blanket, and enjoy your
time together.

What one word would you
use to describe your spouse?

Hers

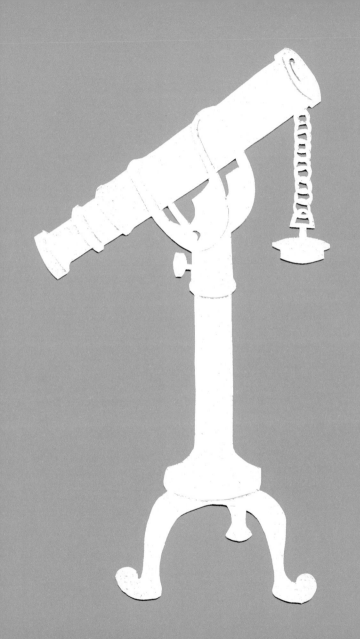

Is there a married couple
in your life that you admire?
Take them out to dinner and
ask for their number one piece
of advice. Record it here.

_____

_____

_____

_____

_____

_____

_____

_____

_____

_____

_____

Take a moment to write
your spouse a love note.
Put it somewhere unexpected.

How long did it take before your spouse found it?

What's on your bucket list as a couple?

_____   /   /

_____   /   /

_____   /   /

_____   /   /

_____   /   /

_____   /   /

_____   /   /

_____   /   /

_____   /   /

_____   /   /

_____   /   /

_____   /   /

_____   /   /

_____   /   /

_____   /   /

_____   /   /

Completed

Therefore encourage
one another and
build one another
up, just as you
are doing.

THE BOOK OF 1 THESSALONIANS

Put away your phones, computers, and TV for the night and pull out a board game or a deck of cards. Or take a walk together.

Does your spouse have a favorite band or musician? Find the closest concert and surprise him or her with tickets and a road trip.

With all humility
and gentleness,
with patience,
bearing with one
another in love,
eager to maintain
the unity of the
Spirit in the
bond of peace.

THE BOOK OF EPHESIANS

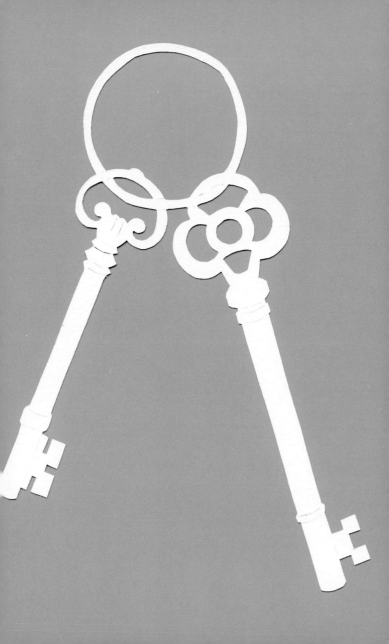

His...

Hers...

Think back to the day you met.
What was the first thing you
noticed about your spouse?

_____

_____

_____

_____

_____

_____

_____

_____

Come on, be honest!

Get in the car and drive with no destination in mind. Just drive and talk the way you did when you first started dating. Stop when you see something you want to eat, drink, or experience.

Maybe check out the world's largest ball of yarn while you are at it.

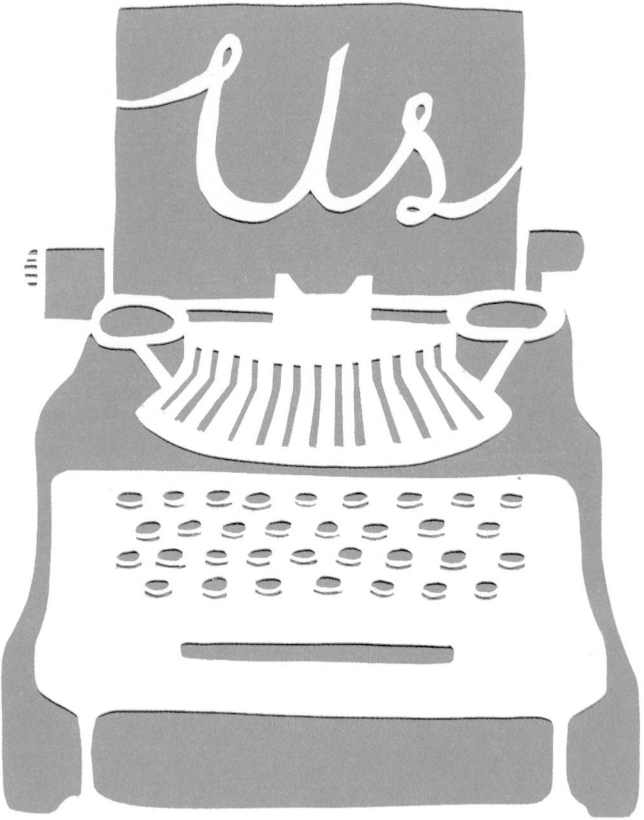
Us

What romance in a book, TV show, or movie is most like your love story?

&

My
heart is,
and always
will be,
yours.

JANE AUSTEN,
SENSE AND SENSIBILITY

DONE ALREADY?

We hope you were able to record some of the special memories that make your story unique. Even better, maybe you were able to spend some intentional time together and make more memories.

The fun doesn't have to stop here. Go back and add to these pages, noting the dates for the different entries. Or start your own memory journal using this book for ideas.

Enjoy your time together—you are writing your love story every day!